German Cookbook

Traditional German Recipes Made Easy

Copyright 2018 by Grizzly Publishing - All rights reserved.

This document is geared towards providing exact and reliable information in regards to the topic and issue covered. The publication is sold with the idea that the publisher is not required to render accounting, officially permitted, or otherwise, qualified services. If advice is necessary, legal or professional, a practiced individual in the profession should be ordered.

- From a Declaration of Principles which was accepted and approved equally by a Committee of the American Bar Association and a Committee of Publishers and Associations.

In no way is it legal to reproduce, duplicate, or transmit any part of this document in either electronic means or in printed format. Recording of this publication is strictly prohibited and any storage of this document is not allowed unless with written permission from the publisher. All rights reserved.

The information provided herein is stated to be truthful and consistent, in that any liability, in terms of inattention or otherwise, by any usage or abuse of any policies, processes, or directions contained within is the solitary and utter responsibility of the recipient reader. Under no circumstances will any legal responsibility or blame be held against the publisher for any reparation, damages, or monetary loss due to the information herein, either directly or indirectly.

Respective authors own all copyrights not held by the publisher.

The information herein is offered for informational purposes solely, and is universal as so. The presentation of the information is without contract or any type of guarantee assurance.

The trademarks that are used are without any consent, and the publication of the trademark is without permission or backing by the trademark owner. All trademarks and brands within this book are for clarifying purposes only and are the owned by the owners themselves, not affiliated with this document.

Introduction

I would like to take this opportunity to thank you for purchasing this book, *"German Cookbook: Traditional German Recipes Made Easy."*

German food is mostly rich, scrumptious and hearty and many top German dishes make great comfort food. Germans love including meat in almost all their meals – sauerbraten, one of the country's national dish is a pot roast (pickled roast that can be made from many different types of meats). The meat or the different varieties of meats are marinated in herbs, wine, spices, seasoning and vinegar for close to 10 days.

Every region in the country has specific traditional cuisine and special dishes. You will find it difficult to choose your top favourite in German cuisine as it can change from one city to the other. The traditional German dinner is known as Abendrot, which translates to evening bread, and includes a wide selection of cheese, whole grain bread, sausages, deli meats and a warm or cold drink. It is impossible to find a German meal without sauerkraut – the German-style fermented cabbage salad. This one dish is rich in multivitamins and probiotics.

You can easily explore the culture of Germany by preparing few traditional German recipes. Not all their dishes are complex to make and many foods are easy to prepare. Incorporating one of these traditional dishes into your weekly meals shouldn't be a tough task. Though the traditional eating habits of Germans have changed over time, there are still a lot of traditional dishes that are simplified and popular across the world. A few of their common and popular dishes are:

- Bratwurst (made of spices and ground pork)
- Blutwurst (blood sausage)
- Wiener (smoked beef or pork cooked in a water bath)
- Schwarzwurst (black sausage made from geese or pigs' blood)

Germans usually have their main meal during the day and then there is a light evening meal between 6 and 7 p.m. Their typical dinner or supper - Abendessen has a combination of bread, meat, sausages, cheese, pickles and mustards. The famous kasespatzle are soft egg noodles that are similar to pasta. Most German meat dishes are accompanied by stews (Garisburger Marsch) and lots of gravy (Rouladen) or sauce.

Sometimes their dishes are served straight from the pan – boiling hot! So, be careful not to burn your mouth! In some regions, they use beer instead of water to mix their dough. Their desserts are simply out of this world – especially the famous Rote Grutze (red fruit pudding made from different types of berries, cherries and currants). Most of their tarts and cakes are made with fresh fruit. It is impossible to resist the temptation to the popular German cake – Schwarzwalder Kirschwasser. Most of their cakes are rich with alternating layers of chocolate, cherries, whipped cream topped with maraschino cherries, chocolate shavings and more cream. Apple strudel is a popular dessert made of buttery pastry with sugar-flavored apples.

You can make your meals interesting even on your busiest day as the best German recipes are not only delicious but also the easiest. Sometimes you just need to step out of your comfort zone to explore the different varieties of food. It is possible for you to make any of these popular German dishes, from the butter dumplings to the yummy butter cakes. Even the rich German meat dishes are not that difficult to prepare.

The German recipes mentioned in the book are mostly traditional and easy to cook. Some of them are the simplified version of their complex ancient method. You don't need to worry about the ingredients, as most of them are quite easily available in the market or in a normal kitchen. You are definitely going to have fun with these recipes. Who knows? You might even invite your friends for an Oktoberfest type setup at your place.

So what are we waiting for? Let us get started cooking the German way. I hope this book serves as an informative and interesting read to you!

Thanks again for purchasing this book. I hope you enjoy it.

Table of Contents

INTRODUCTION .... **V**

CHAPTER ONE: TRADITIONAL GERMAN BREAKFAST RECIPES........................**1**

    GERMAN FARMER'S BREAKFAST 1
    GERMAN PANCAKE 3
    COLORFUL BREAKFAST EGGS 5
    CHOCOLATE OAT MUESLI BAGELS 6
    ONION CAKE (ZWIEBELKUCHEN) 8
    SCHINKEN-SAUERKRAUTROLLEN 10
    MUSHROOM SPAETZLE PAN 12
    SENFEI 13
    EGGS IN GREEN SAUCE 14
    PEPPERONI HOPPLE-POPPLE 15
    FRUITED SAUSAGE 16
    GINGERBREAD PANCAKES 17

CHAPTER TWO: TRADITIONAL GERMAN SOUP RECIPES **18**

    KARTOFFELSUPPE (GERMAN POTATO SOUP) 18
    GOULASH SOUP 20
    GERMAN CABBAGE SOUP 22
    POTATO AND CABBAGE SOUP 24
    GREEN BEAN SOUP 25
    CAULIFLOWER SOUP 26
    BREAD SOUP 28
    CHERVIL SOUP 30
    DARK BEER ONION SOUP 32
    SEVEN HERB SOUP 34

CHAPTER THREE: TRADITIONAL GERMAN SNACKS RECIPES **36**

    CHEESE HEDGEHOG 36
    OPEN-AIR WALDORF SANDWICH 37
    SWEET AND SOUR PICKLED PUMPKIN 39
    SUN-DRIED TOMATO, ENDIVE AND WALNUT SNACKS 41
    SERRANO HAM AND MELON ON WHOLE GRAIN RYE BREAD 42
    SAUSAGE AND SAUERKRAUT PHYLLO TURNOVERS 43
    PIZZA TOAST 45

CHAPTER FOUR: TRADITIONAL GERMAN DUMPLING RECIPES 47

BAVARIAN EGG DUMPLINGS 47
BAVARIAN ZWIEBACK DUMPLINGS 49
POTATO DUMPLINGS FROM THURINGIA 51
CLASSIC GERMAN BREAD DUMPLINGS 53
KARTOFFELKLOESSE 55
SCHUPFNUDELN WITH ORANGE-VANILLA SUGAR 57
GERMAN SPAETZLE DUMPLINGS 59
THÜRINGER KLÖSSE 61

CHAPTER FIVE: TRADITIONAL GERMAN LUNCH RECIPES 63

KARTOFFELPUFFER 63
WILD GARLIC PESTO 64
GERMAN-STYLE CREAMED SPINACH 65
ROULADEN 67
KAESE SPAETZLE 69
SAUERBRATEN 71
KARTOFFELPUFFER 73
CHICKEN PAPRIKASH 74
BASIC BREAD STUFFING 76
CHEESE SPÄTZLE 78
GERMAN NOODLE NESTS 79
EASY ASPARAGUS 81

CHAPTER SIX: TRADITIONAL GERMAN DINNER RECIPES 82

BRATKARTOFFELN 82
BLACK FOREST INN POTATO PURÉE 84
BRAISED RED CABBAGE 85
EDEL-LABSKAUS 87
FRIED ASPARAGUS WITH HERB CREAM 89
HERBED SPAETZLE 91
HORSERADISH-ROASTED FALL VEGETABLES 92
FARMER'S OMELET 93
DIJON-DILL CHICKEN AND NOODLES 95
SAUERKRAUT POTATO PIZZA WITH CAULIFLOWER CRUST 96
CHEESY SPAETZLE WITH VEGETABLES 98
POLISH SAUSAGE SUPPER 100

Potato-Chickpea Patties with Porcini Mushrooms	102
Quinoa Sushi	104
Sausage Skewers with Mango and Bell Pepper	106
Roasted Potatoes	107
Creamed Kohlrabi	108

CHAPTER SEVEN: TRADITIONAL GERMAN DESSERT RECIPES 109

Dark Chocolate Cherry Cupcakes with Kirsch Frosting	109
Hazelnut Crown	111
Marzipan Jubilee Torte	113
Tart Cherry Ice Cream	115
Tangerine Coconut Cake	116
Pumpernickel Ice Cream with Cranberries	117
King of Hearts	118
Fruit Pudding	119
German milchreis	120

CONCLUSION 121

Chapter One: Traditional German Breakfast Recipes

German Farmer's Breakfast

Servings: 4

Ingredients:

- 3 large boiled potatoes (peeled and quartered lengthwise)
- 2 cups white and green onions (roughly chopped) – include the greens in the green onions
- 2 cups ham (chopped)
- 2 cups bell peppers (roughly chopped)
- 1/4 cup parsley (chopped)
- 3 tablespoons olive oil
- 4 eggs (whisked)
- Salt to taste

Method:

1. Heat 2 tablespoons of olive oil in a large skillet over medium-high heat.
2. Add the onions and bell peppers to the heated oil and stir-fry over high heat for 3 minutes until they turn brown
3. Push the fried onions and bell peppers to the side of the pan and add the boiled potatoes (add salt while boiling). Add the remaining olive oil to the skillet
4. Stir-fry for 2 minutes until the potatoes turn golden brown. Sprinkle salt as needed and keep stirring
5. Now add the ham to the potatoes and stir-fry for 2 minutes until the mixture becomes brown

6. Mix all the vegetables (onion, bell peppers, potato) and ham together until combined well
7. Add the parsley and mix again.
8. Now, add the whisked egg and keep stirring until the eggs combine with the vegetables and the ham.
9. Remove from heat when the eggs begin to firm up.
10. Transfer to plate and serve immediately. It goes well with ketchup

German Pancake

Servings: 8

Ingredients:

- 1 cup 2 percent milk
- 6 large eggs
- 2 tablespoons melted butter
- 1 cup all-purpose flour
- 1/2 teaspoon salt

For Buttermilk Syrup:

- 3/4 cup buttermilk
- 2 teaspoons vanilla extract
- 1/2 cup cubed butter
- 2 tablespoons corn syrup
- 1 cups sugar
- Confectioners' sugar
- 1 teaspoon baking soda
- Fresh blueberries

Method:

1. Preheat oven to 400 F
2. Blend 2 percent milk, eggs (crack it), all-purpose flour and salt in a high-speed blender until smooth and creamy
3. Take a 13x9 inches baking dish and pour the melted butter. Tilt to coat the dish (grease it well)
4. Pour the batter in the dish and bake for 20 minutes until it puffs up and turns golden brown (do not cover the baking dish)

5. Heat a small saucepan and add cubed butter, sugar, buttermilk, baking soda and corn syrup. Bring it to boil and cook for 7 minutes uncovered
6. Remove from the heat and add the vanilla extract. Stir the contents well.
7. Remove the baked pancake from oven and dust it with confectioner's sugar
8. Transfer to a plate and serve with the syrup and blueberries.

Colorful Breakfast Eggs

Servings: 4

Ingredients:

- 6 eggs
- 4 cocktail or cherry tomatoes
- 2 tablespoons Emmentaler or Gouda cheese
- 4 ounces genuine Black Forest ham
- 1 bunch watercress
- 1 teaspoon salt

Method:

1. Grate the cheese in a bowl. Add the watercress, two eggs and salt to the grated cheese. Mix the contents until combined thoroughly
2. Take 4 ovenproof glass egg cups (greased) and divide the egg mixture into them.
3. Crack the remaining eggs, place one on each of the cups and close the lids.
4. Fill a shallow sauté pan with simmering water and place the eggcups on the pan with water. The water should reach halfway up the cups.
5. Let the eggs cook for 20 minutes.
6. Transfer the cooked eggs and serve with cocktail tomatoes and ham

Chocolate Oat Muesli Bagels

Servings: 9 bagels

Ingredients:

- 1 cup Kölln Muesli Chocolate and Oats cereal
- 1/2 cup milk (lukewarm)
- 2 cups wheat flour
- 1 egg
- 4 tablespoons butter
- 1 1/2 teaspoon dry yeast
- 2 tablespoons sugar
- 1 pinch Salt

Method:

1. Mix Kölln Muesli Chocolate and Oats cereal, milk, flour, egg (crack it), butter, yeast, sugar and salt in a large bowl. Knead the dough until it stretches easily. Cover the dough for an hour to let it rise.
2. Knead the dough again until you feel the smooth texture and divide it into 9 pieces. Form a ball of each piece and make a 2-inch hole in the middle. Shape the balls into rings and let them sit for 15 minutes (to rise).
3. Pour water into a big pot and add 1 tablespoon of salt. Bring it to boil. Now, place the bagels in the boiling water for 30 seconds. Turn it to the other side and let it be for 30 seconds. Remove carefully and let the rings drain.
4. Line a baking sheet with parchment paper and place the drained bagels on the sheet.

5. Place the sheet on the middle rack of the cold oven and switch it on to 390 F. Bake for 20 minutes until it turns golden brown.
6. Transfer to a plate and serve warm.

Onion Cake (Zwiebelkuchen)

Servings: 2

Ingredients:

- 6 slices Abraham Schwarzwalder Schinken (black forest ham)
- 1 egg yolk
- 2 sliced onions (medium)
- 1 cup sour cream
- 3 cups flour (unbleached)
- 1/4 teaspoon caraway seeds
- 1 cup warm water
- 1 packet active dry yeast
- 1 tablespoon shortening
- 1 tablespoon melted butter
- 1 teaspoon sugar
- 2 teaspoons Salt
- Pepper, as required

Method:

1. Take a bowl and mix 1/2-cup flour, sugar and salt. Add warm water and shortening and beat the mixture for 2 minutes. You can add more flour to make soft dough. Knead the dough for 5 minutes until it has a smooth texture and is able to stretch (should be elastic). Grease another bowl and place the kneaded dough, cover it and place it in a warm place for 30 minutes.
2. Grease a baking sheet or 12-inch pizza pan and pat the dough on it. Press the edges of the dough to form a slight rim.

3. In a skillet, fry the Schwarzwalder Schinken slices in butter until it becomes crispy. Drain the fried slices on absorbent paper.
4. Add the onions to the same skillet and cook until the onions turn translucent and tender.
5. Sprinkle the fried Schwarzwalder Schinken slices, cooked onions, caraway seeds, pepper and 1/2-teaspoon salt over the patted dough in the baking sheet. Bake for 20 minutes at 400 F.
6. Blend the sour cream and egg yolk and pour the mixture over the pre-baked onion cake. Bake again for 15 minutes until the sour cream sets and the cake turns golden brown.
7. Transfer to a plate and serve warm

Schinken-Sauerkrautrollen

Servings: 6

Ingredients:

- 1/3 pound ground pork
- 2 slices bacon
- 1 cup chopped mushrooms
- 1/2 cup tomatoes (crushed)
- 1/4 cup leek (sliced)
- 10 ounces crescent rolls (1 package)
- 3 crushed juniper berries
- 1/2 cup German Emmentaler cheese (shredded)
- 1 cup German wine sauerkraut
- Sour cream, as required
- 1/2 cup cream
- 1 clove

Method:

1. Preheat oven to 375 F. Soak the mushrooms in 1/4 cup cream and cut the bacon slices into cubes.
2. Cook the bacon cubes on high heat in a large shallow skillet and add the ground pork. Let it heat until both the meat are thoroughly cooked. Set it aside to drain the excess grease as it cools.
3. Take a saucepan and add the leek, berries, sauerkraut, tomato and clove. Mix well until combined and simmer for 15 minutes. Add the creamed mushroom and simmer until the mushrooms become soft. Drain the liquid from the mixture and set aside
4. Unroll the crescent roll dough and press the seams together (should form rectangular shape). Cover the

dough with cooked pork and bacon followed by the drained mushroom mixture.
5. Roll the dough into a log and slice them into 6 pieces. Place these 6 slices (should look like cinnamon rolls) on the baking sheet. Sprinkle the shredded cheese over them and pour the remaining cream.
6. Bake for 25 minutes until the rolls turn golden brown. Transfer to place and serve with sour cream. Enjoy!

Mushroom Spaetzle Pan

Servings: 4

Ingredients:

- 1 cup sliced mushrooms
- 4 eggs
- 1/2 cup diced yellow onion
- 4 ounces prepared German spätzle (you can use Bechtel brand or similar ones)
- 1/4 cup chopped fresh parsley
- 2 tablespoons butter (unsalted)
- 1/4 cup cream
- 1/8 teaspoon nutmeg
- 1/4 teaspoon Salt
- 1/8 teaspoon pepper

Method:

1. Beat the eggs in a bowl and add cream, nutmeg, salt and pepper. Mix until combined well and set aside.
2. Heat the butter in a saucepan and cook onion and mushroom over medium heat for 5 minutes until the contents become soft and fragrant.
3. Add the prepared Spaetzle in the saucepan and toast for 3 minutes until it begins to brown. Season with pepper and salt to taste.
4. Add the egg mixture and chopped parsley into the saucepan and cook over low heat. Wait until the eggs are cooked well. Mix the contents and transfer to the plate.
5. Garnish with parsley and serve hot.

Senfei

Servings: 4

Ingredients:

- 8 eggs
- 2 heaping tablespoons all-purpose flour
- 2 cups bouillon or broth
- 1 tablespoon table cream
- 2 tablespoons butter
- 2 tablespoons mustard (German prepared)
- Juice of one lemon
- Salt and pepper to taste
- 1 teaspoon sugar
- 2 cups mashed potatoes

Method:

1. Heat the butter over medium heat in a saucepan. Slowly add the flour and mix with the melted butter as you continue to stir.
2. Add the broth or bouillon slowly and stir the flour-butter mixture. Bring it to boil (don't stop stirring).
3. Add the cream, mustard and sugar to the mixture. Stir constantly. Add salt and pepper to taste.
4. Hard boil the eggs and rinse them in cold water. Peel and cut lengthwise into half. Pour the prepared hot sauce over the eggs. Squeeze the lemon over the sauced eggs.
5. Serve warm with mashed potatoes

Eggs in Green Sauce

Servings: 4

Ingredients:

- 8 eggs
- 2 cups bouillon (broth)
- 2 tablespoons parsley (finely chopped)
- 2 heaping tablespoons all-purpose flour
- 2 tablespoons yogurt (plain)
- 2 tablespoons butter
- 1/2 teaspoon mustard (German prepared)
- 2 tablespoons dill (finely chopped)
- 2 tablespoons watercress
- 2 tablespoons chives (finely chopped)
- Juice of one lemon
- Salt and pepper to taste

Method:

1. Heat the butter over medium heat in a saucepan. Slowly add the flour and mix with the melted butter as you continue to stir.
2. Add the broth or bouillon slowly and stir the flour-butter mixture. Bring it to boil (don't stop stirring).
3. Remove from heat and add the parsley, yogurt, dill, chives, lemon, salt and pepper. Set aside.
4. Hard boil the eggs and rinse them in cold water. Peel and cut lengthwise into half. Pour the prepared cold sauce over the eggs and garnish with watercress.
5. Serve warm with French bread and salad.

Pepperoni Hopple-Popple

Servings: 6

Ingredients:

- 25 slices pepperoni
- 5 eggs (large)
- 2 1/2 cups shredded hash brown potatoes (frozen)
- 1 cup Mexican cheese blend (shredded)
- 1/3 cup onion (chopped)
- 1/2 cup whole milk
- 3 tablespoons butter
- 1 teaspoon Italian seasoning
- 1/2 teaspoon pepper
- 1/2 teaspoon salt

Method:

1. Heat the butter in a large skillet and cook the onions over medium heat until it turns translucent. Add the potatoes and mix well. Cook until the contents turn light brown.
2. In the meantime, take another bowl and beat the eggs, milk, Italian seasoning, pepper and salt together.
3. Pour this beaten egg mixture over the potato-onion mixture and stir well. Sprinkle the pepperoni slices on the mixture.
4. Cover and cook for 12 minutes on medium-low heat until the eggs are set.
5. Remove from heat and sprinkle with shredded cheese. Cover the skillet and let it sit for 2 minutes.
6. Cut it into wedges and transfer to a plate.
7. Serve warm and enjoy!

Fruited Sausage

Servings: 5

Ingredients:

- 16 ounces sliced Fully Cooked Polish Kielbasa Sausage Rope (Johnsonville brand – 1 package)
- 11 ounces drained mandarin oranges (1 can)
- 20 ounces undrained pineapple chunks (1 can)
- 1 cup blueberries (fresh or frozen)
- 2 tablespoons cornstarch
- 1/4 cup brown sugar (packed)

Method:

1. Boil the sausage and pineapple in a large skillet.
2. Add the cornstarch and brown sugar to the skillet. Mix well until combined thoroughly.
3. Add the blueberries and oranges. Bring all the contents to boil. Keep stirring as you cook for 2 more minutes until the contents thicken.
4. Transfer to a plate and serve warm.

Gingerbread Pancakes

Servings: 10

Ingredients:

- 1 egg
- 1 cup all-purpose flour
- 2 tablespoons molasses (black treacle)
- 1 teaspoon ginger (ground)
- 1 cup buttermilk
- 1 tablespoon vegetable oil
- 1/2 teaspoon baking soda
- 1 teaspoon baking powder
- 1/2 teaspoon salt
- 1 tablespoon sugar
- 1/2 teaspoon cinnamon (ground)
- Maple syrup and whipped cream
- Pinch cloves (ground)

Method:

1. Take a large bowl and combine the flour, baking soda, baking powder, salt, sugar, cinnamon, cloves and ginger together.
2. Add the egg (crack it), molasses, buttermilk and oil to the mixture in the bowl. Mix the contents well until it gets a batter consistency.
3. Pour 1/4 cup batter into a hot griddle pan and let it cook. Flip the pancake when bubbles form on the top. Cook until the sides turn golden brown.
4. Repeat step 3 until you finish with the batter.
5. Transfer to a plate and serve with whipped cream and maple syrup.

Chapter Two: Traditional German Soup Recipes

Kartoffelsuppe (German Potato Soup)

Servings: 6

Ingredients:

- 2 pounds waxy potatoes (chopped into 1/4 inch pieces)
- 3 diced carrots
- 1 sliced and thoroughly washed leek (large one)
- 2 diced tomatoes
- 6 cups quality chicken broth
- 8 ounces diced bacon
- 1 large onion (chopped)
- 1 1/2 cups diced celery root
- 1 minced garlic clove
- 1/2 teaspoon dried thyme
- 1/4 cup fresh parsley (chopped)
- 1/2 teaspoon dried rosemary
- 1/2 teaspoon black pepper (freshly ground)
- 1/2 teaspoon dried sage or marjoram
- 3/4 teaspoon sea salt
- 1 bay leaf
- 3 tablespoons olive oil

Method:

1. Heat the oil in a large pot (or skillet) over medium-high heat.
2. Add the bacon to the hot oil and fry it.

3. Add the onion to the pot and continue to stir-fry for 8 minutes until it turns golden brown.
4. Add the garlic to the mixture and let it cook for one more minute as you continue stirring the contents
5. Now, add the potatoes, carrots, leek, tomatoes, celery root and bay life. Mix well until combined
6. Add the thyme, rosemary, pepper, marjoram and bay leaf. Stir the contents to make sure the flavors blend well.
7. Pour the chicken broth into the pot and add salt to the contents. Mix well until well incorporated.
8. Bring it to boil and cover the pot. Reduce the heat to medium-low and let it simmer for 40 minutes
9. Finally, add the chopped parsley and allow it to simmer for one more minute. Add more salt and pepper (if desired)
10. Turn off heat, transfer to a bowl and serve hot!
11. You can store the soup for the next day as the flavor gets better making it an excellent make-ahead soup.

Goulash Soup

Servings: 6

Ingredients:

- 1 pound stewing beef (chopped into ¾-inch cubes)
- 1 cup beef broth
- 3 diced potatoes
- 2 coarsely diced onions
- 3 peppers (1 red, 1 yellow, 1 green), cut into 1-inch pieces
- 1 crushed garlic clove
- 1 tablespoon Hungarian paprika (sweet)
- 1 1/2 cups tomato juice
- 2 tablespoons olive oil
- 1 teaspoon salt
- 1 teaspoon freshly ground black pepper (seasoning)

Method:

1. Heat the oil over medium-high heat in a large pot. Add half the stewing beef and stir-fry it until completely browned
2. Remove the cooked meat from the pot and set aside.
3. Brown the remaining stewing beef (*if needed, you can adjust the heat consistency*)
4. Once the meat is done, add the already cooked beef back to the pot.
5. Add onions and garlic and continue to cook for 20 minutes as you continue to stir often
6. Pour the beef broth and tomato juice into the pot. Stir well.

7. Add paprika and salt to the mixture as you keep stirring continuously.
8. Bring it to boil, cover the pot and reduce the heat to medium-low. Allow it to simmer and cook for another 40 minutes
9. Add the peppers (red, green, yellow) and potatoes to the pot, cook for additional 15 minutes until the potatoes become soft and tender
10. Season with black pepper if you like it hot.
11. Transfer to a bowl and serve hot.

German Cabbage Soup

Servings: 4

Ingredients:

- 3 pounds shredded cabbage
- 1 pound ground beef
- 2 1/2 pounds potatoes
- 2 diced medium onions,
- 4 cups chicken broth (or bouillon cubes)
- 1 tablespoon vinegar
- 2 tablespoon olive oil
- 2 teaspoons salt
- 1/4 teaspoon pepper
- 2 tablespoons caraway seeds
- 1 tablespoon Maggi Seasoning Sauce (optional)

Method:

1. No need to peel the potatoes if they are fresh and have thin skin. Slice them into bite-sized pieces.
2. Heat oil in a large pot over medium-high heat. Add the onions to the hot oil and cook for 3 minutes until translucent
3. Add the ground beef to the pot and continue to cook for 20 minutes until the meat is completely browned (adjust the heat accordingly)
4. Add a splash of water and stir the contents to check if there are any browned bits stuck to the bottom.
5. Now, add the potatoes and cabbage. Add the chicken broth until it covers about 1 inch below the level of the veggies. (*Adding water one inch above the veggies*

will result in a more liquid-like soup – too much liquid)
6. Add the salt, caraway seeds and pepper now. Stir the contents and bring it to boil.
7. Cover the pot and simmer for 60 to 90 minutes stirring frequently as the soup gets cooked
8. Add the seasoning and vinegar finally. Heat it through for 1 more minute
9. Transfer to a bowl and serve hot.

Potato and Cabbage Soup

Servings: 4

Ingredients:

- 1 pound diced potatoes
- 1 pound shredded savoy or green cabbage
- 1/2 pound sliced leeks (thoroughly washed and drained)
- 1/2 pound sliced carrots
- 1 1/2 quarts vegetable broth
- 1 diced small onion
- Smoked sausage (1 ring)
- 1 tablespoon chopped parsley
- 1 teaspoon salt
- 1/2 teaspoon pepper
- 2 tablespoons olive oil

Method:

1. Heat the oil over medium-high heat in a large pot. Add the onions and sauté for 3-4 minutes until translucent.
2. Add the cabbage to the pot and cook for another 5 minutes until brown.
3. Add the leeks and carrots to the pot, continue to cook stirring the contents often
4. Pour the broth into the pot, add salt and pepper as you continue cooking.
5. Bring it to boil, cover the pot and simmer for 30 minutes until the vegetables become soft.
6. Reduce the heat to medium-low and add the smoked sausage to the soup as it simmers.

7. Sprinkle the parsley over the soup and serve hot!

Green Bean Soup

Servings: 4

Ingredients:

- 2 pounds green beans (frozen)
- 5 boiled potatoes (chopped)
- 1 pound lean ground beef
- 1 chopped medium onion
- 2 tablespoons food seasoning (Vegeta brand)
- 2 tablespoons oil

Method:

1. Heat oil in a large pot over medium-high heat
2. Add ground beef to the hot oil and stir-fry until browned
3. Add the onions and cook for 3 minutes until translucent and turns light brown
4. Add the frozen beans and cook for 5-7 minutes until the beans are thoroughly cooked
5. Add the boiled potatoes and give it a stir.
6. Pour water into the pot until it covers the veggies by an inch and add the food seasoning.
7. Bring it to boil and reduce the heat to medium-low. Cover the pot, simmer and cook for 30 minutes.
8. When the flavor springs up, turn off the heat and transfer to the serving bowl.
9. Serve and enjoy!

Cauliflower Soup

Servings: 4

Ingredients:

- 1 small cauliflower (about 1 pound)
- 6 tablespoons cornstarch flour
- 3 tablespoons 10 percent cream
- 1 egg yolk
- 3 tablespoons butter
- 1 teaspoon pepper
- 2 teaspoons salt

Method:

1. Wash the cauliflower and trim it by removing the thick stems. Cut into small florets and drain the water.
2. Take a medium-sized pot and place the cauliflower florets in it. Pour water until it covers the florets and add 1 teaspoon salt. Stir it once.
3. Bring it to boil, cover the pot and reduce the heat.
4. Simmer and cook for 15 minutes until the florets become tender
5. Remove from heat and allow it to cool. Drain the florets into a sieve and reserve the drained liquid
6. Heat the butter over medium heat in the same pot until it melts.
7. Add the flour and continue to stir. Cook it for a minute but don't let it brown.
8. Pour 4 cups of the hot liquid (drained from cauliflower) to the pot and bring it to boil
9. Simmer for 10 minutes and remove from heat

10. Take a small bowl and pour the egg yolk. Add the cream to the yolk and mix it together
11. Pour 1/4 cup of the hot soup (the flour liquid from steps 8 and 9) to the egg-cream mixture to *temper* it.
12. Pour this egg-cream mixture to the pot and add the cooked cauliflower to it. Season it with salt and pepper.
13. Blend the soup using an immersion blender to get a smooth creamy texture
14. Transfer to a bowl and serve hot.

Bread Soup

Servings: 4 - 6

Ingredients:

- 6 slices hearty wheat bread (cut into cubes)
- 1 1/2 ounces Allgäuer Emmentaler cheese
- 4 tablespoons butter
- 4 ounces ham (chopped)
- 3 cups beef broth
- 1 bunch chives (chopped)
- 2 egg yolks
- 1/2 cup cream

Method:

1. Heat 3 tablespoons butter in a pot over medium heat until melted
2. Add 3/4th of the bread cubes to the melted butter and fry them.
3. Pour the beef broth and bring it to boil.
4. Reduce the heat to the lowest and carefully whisk the contents in the pot until smooth (use a hand blender)
5. Take a small bowl and whisk together the egg, cream and cheese until well-blended.
6. Add this mixture to the pot and stir well until the contents are incorporated
7. Add the chopped ham and chives to the soup and let it simmer for some more time.
8. Meanwhile, heat another saucepan and melt the remaining butter over medium heat. Fry the remaining bread cubes until golden brown

9. Sprinkle this fried bread cubes over the soup in the pot. Turn off the heat.
10. Transfer to a bowl and serve hot!

Chervil Soup

Servings: 5 - 6

Ingredients:

- 2 bunches fresh chervil
- 13 1/2 fluid ounce chicken stock (1.5 cups)
- 4 hard-boiled eggs
- 2 beaten egg yolks
- 1/2 cup crème Fraiche
- 2 spring onions (washed and sliced)
- 8 1/2 fluid ounce cream (1 cup)
- 1 tablespoon butter
- 1 teaspoon lemon juice
- Salt and freshly ground pepper, to taste
- A pinch of sugar

Method:

1. Wash the chervil, remove the stems and pat dry. Chop the leaves finely and reserve few stems for garnishing.
2. Heat butter in a pot over medium heat and fry the spring onions in it.
3. Add the broth, crème Fraiche and cream to the pot. Stir well until combined.
4. Bring it to boil and reduce the heat. Add lemon juice, salt, pepper and sugar. Give the contents a good mix.
5. Add the chopped chervil and simmer for 5-7 minutes (don't let the soup to boil)
6. Whisk the egg yolks in a small bowl and add it to the pot. Continue to cook until the raw flavor goes and the mixture blends in.

7. Turn off the heat and pour the soup into a serving bowl. Cut the hard-boiled eggs into half and place it in the center of the soup.
8. Sprinkle the chervil steps over it and serve hot. (Repeat for the remaining soup)

Dark Beer Onion Soup

Servings: 4

Ingredients:

- 1 cup dark beer (German Dark Oktoberfest Bier)
- 4 onions (peeled and cut into rings)
- 4 Zwieback toasts (Brandt Zwieback brand)
- 3 tablespoons chives (chopped)
- 4 cups beef broth
- 4 tablespoons butter
- Salt and pepper, to taste

Method:

1. Heat 2 tablespoons butter in a pot over medium heat. Add the onion rings and sauté for 3-4 minutes until translucent and tender.
2. Pour the broth into the pot and season it with pepper and salt.
3. Bring it to boil, reduce the heat and simmer the contents for 10 minutes.
4. Meanwhile, soak the zwieback toasts in the dark beer for few minutes.
5. Take another frying pan and heat the remaining butter over medium heat.
6. Fry the beer-soaked toast in the butter until golden brown. Flip the sides and fry until golden.
7. Turn off the heat and remove the pot. Transfer the soup to a bowl and top it with the fried toasts and chopped chives.
8. Serve hot and enjoy!

Note: If you do not want beer in your soup, you can skip step 4 and fry the zwieback with onion powder and celery. Top it with cheese and grill before adding it to the soup.

Seven Herb Soup

Servings: 4

Ingredients:

- Fresh herbs (Ramps, nettles, parsley, tarragon, chives, spring onions, watercress and salad burnet).
- 2 cups vegetable broth
- 2 chopped small potatoes (boiled and peeled)
- 1 finely chopped small onion
- Cubed zwieback or croutons (for garnishing)
- 1 tablespoon butter
- Edible flowers such as violets or dandelions (for garnishing)
- 1 tablespoon cornstarch flour
- Salt and pepper, to taste
- 1 teaspoon chopped chives (for garnishing)

Method:

1. If the herbs are from your garden, pick them up early in the morning.
2. Wash the herbs thoroughly in running water, drain them and dry a bit. Chop the herbs coarsely such that you get 2 handfuls of the chopped herbs (for a person)
3. Heat the butter in a pot over medium heat. Add onion and sauté for 3 minutes until translucent and tender
4. Add the cornstarch flour and stir well. Let it cook for some time but don't brown it.
5. Pour the vegetable stock and mix the contents well. Bring it to boil and reduce the heat to low.

6. Simmer the mixture for 3 minutes and add the boiled potatoes. Give it a stir and add the herbs now. Increase the heat to medium-high and bring it to boil.
7. Season the soup with salt and pepper. Use a hand blender and puree it to form a thick, creamy consistency
8. Transfer it to a serving bowl. Garnish with edible flowers, chives and croutons.
9. Serve warm and enjoy!

Chapter Three: Traditional German Snacks Recipes

Cheese Hedgehog

Servings: 2-3

Ingredients:

- 1 cup white and red grapes (seedless)
- 1/2 cup Allgäuer Emmentaler cheese (or Tilsit cheese or Butterkäse cheese)
- 1/2 melon or muskmelon

Method

1. Slice the cheese into cubes and set aside
2. Place the melon in a big plate with its flat side facing down on the plate.
3. Insert a wooden toothpick into the cheese cubes, white grape and red grape alternatively (first insert cheese cube, then the white grape and then red grape; take the next toothpick, insert white grape, cheese cube, red grape, etc.)
4. You can choose to insert the fruits and cheese as you wish.
5. Now, stick the grape and cheese toothpicks into the round side of fruit.
6. Get creative and make it colorful (by using different fruits of your choice, if you desire)
7. When you are done, you get a cool cheese hedgehog
8. Relish and enjoy!

Open-Air Waldorf Sandwich

Servings: 4

Ingredients:

- 8 slices white sandwich bread
- 2 ounces German Emmental cheese
- 1/2 pound celery stalks with leaves (washed, cleaned and finely chopped – chop the stalks and leaves separately)
- 3 thin-sliced small tomatoes (firm ones)
- 2 tablespoons finely chopped pumpkin seeds
- 6 tablespoons salad cream light mayonnaise
- Salt and pepper, to taste

Method

1. Spread around 4 tablespoons of salad cream light mayonnaise to all the 8 bread slices.
2. Cut a 4-inch round out of each slice and slice the rounds into half to get half moons. Place the 16 half moons in a plate and set aside.
3. Slice the cheese into small cubes and set aside.
4. Take a small bowl and combine the celery stalks, pumpkin seeds, cheese and the remaining salad cream. Add some salt and pepper, mix well and keep ready
5. Place the celery leaves on the half moon bread piece, layer it with the tomato slice, spread the celery salad and place another half moon bread piece on top. Again, place the celery leaves on top of that bread piece and repeat the layering process.

6. You can place four layers of bread slices. Repeat the step 5 with the remaining half moon bread pieces
7. Garnish with celery leaves and serve immediately

Sweet and Sour Pickled Pumpkin

Servings: 1 large jar

Ingredients:

- 2 pounds firm pumpkin meat (chopped into large cubes)
- 1.6 pounds preserving sugar
- 1 cup wine vinegar
- 6 whole cloves
- 1 cup water
- 1 cinnamon stick
- Grated zest of 1 organic lemon
- 1/2 teaspoon ginger (ground)
- 1 bay leaf

Method

1. Place the pumpkin meat cubes in a large pot.
2. Pour 1 cup water in a smaller pot and add vinegar to it. Boil the water over medium heat.
3. Pour the boiling water-vinegar mixture over the pumpkin cubes in the large pot. Cover the pot and let it sit for 12 hours
4. After 12 hours, take off the pumpkin cubes and boil the water-vinegar mixture again.
5. Add sugar, cloves, cinnamon stick, ginger and bay leaf to the boiling vinegar mixture.
6. Add the pumpkin now and let it continue to boil until the pumpkin pieces become translucent.
7. Using a large spoon, remove the pumpkin pieces again and transfer them into large preserving glass jars.

8. Carefully remove the cloves, cinnamon stick and bay leaf from the vinegar-sugar concoction.
9. Reduce the heat and continue to simmer until the liquid reduces.
10. Pour this hot mixture over the pumpkin cubes in the jar until they are completely submerged in it.
11. Close the jar tightly and store. Serve whenever you like!

Sun-Dried Tomato, Endive and Walnut Snacks

Servings: 2

Ingredients:

- 2 ounces sun-dried tomatoes (chopped into small pieces)
- 1 head endive
- 1 ounce walnuts (coarsely chopped)
- Mestemacher Mixed Cereal Bread
- 3 tablespoons butter
- 3 finely chopped sage leaves
- 3.5 ounces cream cheese (mushroom flavor)
- Pepper, to taste

Method

1. Take a small bowl and place the chopped tomatoes and sage leaves in it.
2. Add the mushroom flavored cream cheese over the tomatoes and sage leaves and mix well.
3. Separate the endive leaves from the stem and set aside
4. Toast the mixed cereals bread and spread the butter lightly on each slice.
5. Place the endive leaves on the slice, spread the tomato-sage-cheese mixture over the leaves and sprinkle the chopped walnuts and pepper on it.
6. Place another buttered bread slice and serve.

Serrano Ham and Melon on Whole Grain Rye Bread

Servings: 4

Ingredients:

- 5.5 ounces thin-sliced Serrano ham
- 4 slices Mestemacher Whole Grain Rye Bread
- 1 bouquet of parsley (cleaned and finely chopped)
- 1/2 Crenshaw melon or Galia
- Crushed pink peppercorn, to taste

Method

1. Chop the melon into oblong pieces and place one piece each on the ham slices.
2. Roll the ham around the melon and place it on top of the bread slice
3. Sprinkle the chopped parsley over it and some pepper to taste
4. Place another bread slice on top of it and serve.

Sausage and Sauerkraut Phyllo Turnovers

Servings: 12 turnovers

Ingredients:

- 2 grilled and chopped Bockwurst sausages (or Bratwurst)
- 4 10x12-inch large sheets phyllo dough
- 10 ounces drained and rinsed sauerkraut
- 5.5 tablespoons melted butter
- 2.75 ounces Bavarian smoked cheese (chopped roughly in small pieces)

Method

1. Cut the dough sheets end-to-end in 3 pieces and use a cling film to cover them so they don't dry out.
2. Take a big flat plate or a cutting board and place the dough strip. Brush it with melted butter and place a heaped teaspoon of sauerkraut in one end of the strip (corner end)
3. Place the chopped sausage on top of it and press lightly. Put 3-4 cheese cubes and fold the phyllo sheet diagonally by wrapping the filling so it gets completely enclosed in a triangle.
4. Flip over again on the diagonal and repeat until you get to the end of the phyllo strip to form a neat triangular turnover.
5. Place them on a flat baking sheet and repeat steps 2 to 4 with the remaining ingredients until you get 12 turnovers.
6. Preheat the oven to 400 degrees F

7. Brush the sides and tops of the turnovers with the remaining butter and bake for 15 minutes until crisp and golden.
8. Serve warm and enjoy!

Pizza Toast

Servings:

Ingredients:

- 3.5 ounces thinly sliced pepperoni and ham
- 8 sandwich bread slices
- 4 tomatoes
- 1.75 ounces Gouda cheese (v)
- 16 fresh basil leaves
- 2 teaspoons mild paprika
- 1 mozzarella ball
- 2 tablespoons canola oil
- Salt and pepper, to taste

Method

1. Wash the tomatoes and slice them into round shape. Set aside.
2. Wash the basil leaves and pat them dry. Set aside.
3. Cut the mozzarella balls into slices and set aside.
4. Preheat the oven to 300 degrees F
5. Place the bread slices on a parchment-lined baking sheet. Drizzle the slices with canola oil
6. Divide the ham and pepperoni slices evenly among the bread slices.
7. Place the tomato slices on top of them and season with salt and pepper.
8. Place 2 basil leaves over each slice of bread.
9. Place mozzarella slices on 4 bread slices and grated cheese on the other 4 bread slices
10. Sprinkle the entire bread slices with paprika and bake for 20 minutes until crispy

11. Transfer to a plate and serve warm!

Chapter Four: Traditional German Dumpling Recipes

Bavarian Egg Dumplings

Servings: 7 dumplings

Ingredients:

- 1 package Panni Bavarian Potato Dumpling Mix (6.8 ounces)
- 1 egg
- 1 slice soft roll bread
- 2 cups water
- 2 tablespoons parsley (chopped)
- 4 tablespoons margarine or butter
- Nutmeg
- Salt

Method:

1. Cut the soft roll bread into small cubes and set aside
2. Heat the margarine in a small saucepan over medium heat. Add the roll bread cubes in the hot oil and fry them until golden brown.
3. Crack the egg into a mixing bowl and stir well.
4. Add the fried soft roll bread cubes, chopped parsley, nutmeg and salt to the bowl. Add a bit of water and mix gently.
5. Add the dumpling powder to the bowl and mix it well with your hands adjusting consistency (not so thick not so thin)
6. Let the dough sit for 20 minutes.

7. Pour water in a pot and add salt (as per your taste) to it. Let it boil.
8. Meanwhile moisten your hands and form 7 dumplings using the dough.
9. Place them carefully in the boiling salt water. Let it boil for less than a minute and reduce the heat to low heat.
10. Allow it to simmer for 10 minutes.
11. When the dumplings are ready, transfer it to a plate and serve warm

Bavarian Zwieback Dumplings

Servings: 4

Ingredients:

- 16 Zwieback toasts (1 pack – Brandt brand)
- 2 eggs
- 1 medium size onion (peeled and finely diced)
- 1 1/2 cups milk
- 4 tablespoons parsley (chopped)
- 2 tablespoons all-purpose flour
- Salt
- 1 tablespoon butter

Method:

1. Crumble 4 zwieback toasts finely and set aside. Place the remaining zwieback toasts into a large bowl
2. Heat milk in a shallow saucepan over medium heat. Don't boil or overheat, lukewarm should do. Add a pinch of salt to the lukewarm milk and pour it over the zwieback toasts in the large bowl. Allow it to soak for 20 minutes
3. Take another frying pan and heat the butter until it melts.
4. Add the onion to the melted butter and sauté for 2-3 minutes until translucent and soft. Set it aside.
5. Go back to the soaked toasts and crack the eggs to the bowl, add the cooked onion, chopped parsley, flour and zwieback crumbs.
6. Stir the contents until you get smooth dough. Make sure the contents are thoroughly combined and you

don't have any lumps. Let this dough sit for 20 minutes.
7. Boil water with a pinch of salt (add more if needed) in a pot.
8. Moisten your hands and form dumplings. Cook them in the boiling water for 20 minutes.
9. Drain and transfer to serving plate.
10. Serve hot

Potato Dumplings from Thuringia

Servings: 4

Ingredients:

- 4 pounds washed and peeled starchy potatoes (Idaho or Russet)
- 1 Kaiser roll or dry bread
- 1 tablespoon butter
- Shot of vinegar
- 1 cup of croutons
- Salt

Method:

1. Take a large bowl and fill it with lukewarm water. Add a shot of vinegar to the water.
2. Grate 2/3rd of the potatoes and put the grated potatoes in the vinegar water.
3. Strain the grated potatoes by pouring out the water carefully. Add new water and a shot of vinegar and repeat the process once again.
4. Spread a cloth dish towel or cheesecloth and place the grated potato in it.
5. Squeeze out the liquid from the grated potato and reserve the liquid in a bowl (the starch of the potato will settle onto the bottom of the bowl).
6. Leave the potatoes in the dish towel itself and set aside.
7. Remove the crust from the Kaiser roll and dice it small.

8. Heat the butter in a frying pan and sauté the Kaiser roll cubes in the melted butter until it turns golden brown.
9. Boil the remaining potatoes in salted water (lightly salted) until soft and tender.
10. Once boiled, drain the potato leaving some liquid in the pot used for boiling. Mash the potatoes in the same pot until creamy and puree-consistency.
11. Boil this potato puree.
12. Now, drain the reserved liquid carefully from the bowl until only the starch remains in the bowl.
13. Add a pinch of salt and the grated potatoes to the starch. Mix well until combined.
14. Slowly add the boiled potato puree and incorporate it well with the mixture using a hand blender. Beat the mixture well (you will see it coming off the sides of the bowl)
15. When the dough is ready, moisten your hands and make round dumplings. Take 2 croutons and press it to the center of each dumpling.
16. Simmer water in a pot and carefully place the dumpling in it (boiling water might break the dumplings).
17. Cook on low heat for 30 minutes. Drain and transfer to a serving plate.
18. Serve and enjoy!

Classic German Bread Dumplings

Servings: 4

Ingredients:

- 8 day-old white buns or white bread slices
- 1 peeled and chopped onion
- 2 eggs
- 1 cup 2% milk (heated)
- 2 tablespoons dumplings mix or all-purpose flour
- 1 teaspoon butter
- 2 handfuls chopped fresh parsley
- Pinch of salt

Method:

1. If you are using the buns, cut them into thin slices and put them in a bowl. Pour the warm milk into the bowl over the sliced buns or bread slices. Let it soak for 10-15 minutes.
2. Heat butter in a frying pan over medium heat. Add onions when the butter melts and sauté for 2-3 minutes until golden brown. Turn off heat and set aside to cool.
3. Take a large bowl and crack the eggs. Add the flour, parsley, salt, soaked bread slices or buns and fried onions to the bowl. Knead the mixture to form smooth dough.
4. Boil water with a pinch of salt in a large pot.
5. Moisten your hands and form 10 dumplings of equal size. Place them carefully in the boiling water and reduce the heat. Let it simmer for 15 minutes

6. The dumplings are ready when you see them floating in the water surface and gently rotating. Check if the texture is firm and remove them from water
7. Transfer to a plate and serve warm

Kartoffelkloesse

Servings: 6

Ingredients:

- 2 slices sourdough bread or white bread
- 2 scrubbed and unpeeled large russet potatoes (about 1 1/2 pounds)
- 1 large egg
- 1/8 cup cornstarch or potato starch
- 1/2 cup all-purpose flour
- 1/8 teaspoon nutmeg (ground)
- 1 tablespoon corn oil or vegetable oil
- 1 1/2 teaspoons salt
- 1 tablespoon butter (unsalted)

Method:

1. Remove the crusts from the bread and reserve. Slice the bread into 1/2 inch cubes and set aside.
2. Heat butter and corn oil in a saucepan over medium heat and fry the bread in the hot butter-oil mixture until golden brown.
3. Transfer the fried bread cubes to a paper towel to drain the excess oil
4. Boil the potatoes in a large pot of water with a pinch of salt for about 30 to 45 minutes until soft and tender
5. Drain the potatoes and let it cool. Peel them and slice them into large chunks. Refrigerate the potato chunks for 30 minutes until it becomes cold.
6. Take a large bowl and mash the potatoes nicely with a fork.

7. Add nutmeg, salt, cornstarch or potato starch and half flour to the mashed potatoes.
8. Use your hands and knead it to soft dough. If the dough is too sticky, add more flour and knead it to a thick consistency.
9. Crack the eggs in and mix well to form smooth dough. Let it sit for 10 minutes.
10. Moisten your hands and form a ball from the dough.
11. Insert a fried bread cube to the center of the ball and roll it again between your palms to enclose the fried bread cube fully. Form smooth dumplings.
12. Boil water with a pinch of salt in a large pot and place them in the boiling water.
13. Simmer for 10 minutes until the dumplings are cooked. Once they float on the surface of the water, remove and transfer to a plate. (*Place only 4 or 5 dumplings at a time in the boiling water*).
14. Serve warm and enjoy!

Schupfnudeln with Orange-Vanilla Sugar

Servings: 10

Ingredients:

- 3 medium russet potatoes
- 1 large egg (beaten)
- Finely minced zest of 3 oranges
- 1/2 cup all-purpose flour (plus extra for dusting)
- 1 cup granulated sugar
- 1 tablespoon vegetable oil
- 1/2 teaspoon kosher salt
- 1 scraped vanilla bean

Method:

1. Boil the potatoes until soft and tender. Drain the boiled potatoes and let it cool.
2. Meanwhile, place the minced orange zest in a microwave-safe plate lined with paper towel. Microwave the zest for 4 minutes taking 30-seconds interval until it is brittle and dry.
3. Transfer the dried zest to a food processor, add the scraped vanilla bean and granulated sugar.
4. Pulse the contents until sugar becomes powdery with bits of orange zest and vanilla bean throughout. Transfer to a large mixing bowl.
5. Peel the boiled potatoes and cut them into chunks (1-inch size). Mash them using a fork in a large bowl.
6. Add the beaten egg, flour and salt to the mashed potatoes. Knead well using your hands to form smooth dough.

7. Place the dough in a lightly-floured surface and roll it into a rectangle (10x8 inch spread with ½-inch thickness).
8. Use a bench scraper and cut the dough into half lengthwise and then again cut it across widthwise. Make 34 rectangles with 1/2-inch sections and roll them using your hands into dumplings 6-inch long with tapered ends
9. Line a baking sheet with parchment and dust it with flour. Place the dumplings on the tray and let it rest for 15 minutes in room temperature.
10. Fill a large Dutch oven with 2 inches of oil. Bring it to 375 degrees F over medium-high heat and fry the dumplings in batches for 5 minutes until it becomes crispy and golden brown.
11. Transfer the fried dumplings to a baking sheet lined with paper towel for the excel oil to drain.
12. Now, toss these hot fried dumplings in the orange-vanilla mixture in the bowl until it is completely coated.
13. Serve immediately and enjoy!

German Spaetzle Dumplings

Servings: 6

Ingredients:

- 1 cup all-purpose flour
- 2 eggs (beaten)
- 1/4 cup milk
- 2 tablespoons fresh parsley (chopped)
- 2 tablespoons butter
- 1/2 teaspoon nutmeg (ground)
- 16 cups hot water
- 1 pinch white pepper (freshly ground)
- 1/2 teaspoon salt

Method:

1. Take a large bowl and combine the flour, nutmeg, white pepper and salt until well-combined.
2. Add the beaten eggs to the bowl and add milk slowly while you knead the mixture to form smooth dough.
3. Pour the hot water into a large pot and simmer over low heat
4. Press the dough through a large-holed sieve or Spaetzle maker. Drop few at a time into the simmering hot liquid.
5. Let it cook for 8 minutes and remove from the pot when they float on the surface.
6. Transfer the cooked Spaetzle to a plate.
7. Heat butter in a large saucepan over medium heat and sauté the cooked Spaetzle in the melted butter.
8. Transfer to a plate and sprinkle the fresh parsley on top.

9. Serve and enjoy!

Thüringer Klösse

Servings: 4-6

Ingredients:

- 2 pounds starchy potatoes (peeled)
- 4 bread slices (one-day old)
- 5 tablespoons semolina cream
- 4 tablespoons butter
- 1 cup milk
- 2 teaspoon salt

Method:

1. Cut the bread slices into cubes and fry them in 2 tablespoons of butter to make croutons.
2. Grate the peeled potatoes into a pan of cold water. When you are done grating the potatoes, put them into cheesecloth and squeeze out the liquid (as much as possible). Transfer the drained grated potato into a bowl.
3. Boil milk in a pot over medium-high heat and add semolina cream, 2 tablespoons of butter and 1 teaspoon of water to it.
4. Reduce the heat and simmer. Keep stirring as it simmers until the milk mixture forms a ball and starts leaving the sides of the pan.
5. Add this creamy wheat mixture to the grated potatoes in the bowl. Knead to form smooth dough.
6. Dust your hands with flour and form dumplings (the size of a potato) and press the 2 croutons (fried bread cubes) to the center of the dumpling.

7. Boil water in a large pot and place the dumplings careful in the boiling water.
8. Simmer for 15 minutes and remove the cooked dumplings when they begin to float on the surface of the water.
9. Transfer to a plate and serve hot!

Chapter Five: Traditional German Lunch Recipes

Kartoffelpuffer

Servings: 4

Ingredients:

- 3 pounds potatoes (peeled and washed)
- 2 eggs (beaten)
- 2 onions (finely chopped)
- Salt & pepper, to taste
- 3 tablespoons olive oil
- Applesauce, for serving

Method:

1. Grate the potatoes using a box grater and place it in cheesecloth. Strain the grated potatoes and remove liquid as much as possible.
2. Take a bowl and place the onion in it. Add the grated potato, beaten eggs, salt and pepper to the bowl.
3. Mix well until the contents are blended well to form a dough-like consistency.
4. Heat the oil in a frying pan over medium-high heat. Using a small ladle, spoon the mixture and flatten it a bit.
5. Place it on the hot oil and fry until golden brown. Flip it to the other side and continue frying until crispy and brown.
6. Transfer to a plate and serve hot with applesauce.

Wild Garlic Pesto

Servings: 4

Ingredients:

- 3 ounces wild garlic ramps
- 3 tablespoons grated parmesan cheese
- 1/4 cup rapeseed oil or canola oil (cold-pressed)
- 2 tablespoons pine nuts
- Salt and pepper, to taste

Method

1. Rinse the wild garlic ramps thoroughly under running water. Drain them well and chop coarsely.
2. Take a food processor and place the chopped wild garlic ramps, cheese, rapeseed oil and pine nuts into it.
3. Pulse for 60 seconds until the mixture becomes a smooth paste.
4. Transfer to a bowl and season it with pepper and salt.
5. Mix it with a spoon and serve!

German-Style Creamed Spinach

Servings: 6

Ingredients:

- 2.5 cups frozen spinach, thawed
- 1 finely diced small yellow onion (you will get about 1 cup)
- 2 cups aged Gouda cheese (grated)
- 3 tablespoons butter (unsalted)
- Kosher salt and freshly ground pepper, to taste
- 1/8 teaspoon nutmeg (freshly grated)
- 1 1/2 cups heavy cream

Method

1. Thaw the frozen spinach and strain through a colander.
2. Wrap the drained spinach in a cheesecloth or cloth towel and squeeze out the liquid from the spinach.
3. Heat butter over medium heat in a large skillet (straight-sided one) and add the onions to the melted butter.
4. Stir-fry the onions for 8 minutes until translucent and tender. Add kosher salt and pepper. Mix well.
5. Add the grated nutmeg and heavy cream to the skillet; continue to cook for 3 minutes until the cream gets reduced by half.
6. Add the grated cheese to the creamy onion mixture and stir until the cheese melts.
7. Now, add the spinach and mix well until the flavors blend and the mixture is well-incorporated.

8. Cover the skillet and cook for 10 minutes over medium-low heat until the spinach becomes soft and tender.
9. Add more salt and pepper as desired. Mix well for one last time and transfer to a bowl.
10. Serve warm and enjoy!

Rouladen

Servings: 10

Ingredients:

- 3 3/4 pounds thinly sliced (1/4 inch) chuck roast (10 strips)
- 1/4 cup cornstarch
- 15 strips of bacon
- 1 thinly sliced large onion
- 1 teaspoon yellow mustard paste
- 1 teaspoon pepper (freshly ground)
- 3 cups water, divided
- 1/2 cup vegetable oil
- 1 teaspoon sea salt
- Sour cream, optional

Method:

1. Spread a thin layer of mustard paste on the chuck roast strips and sprinkle pepper and salt over it.
2. Put one or two strips of bacon on the meat (ensure the bacon doesn't stick out in the side). Cover the bacon with sliced onions (thin layer should do).
3. Start rolling the meat from the small end along with its contents to form a tight cylinder.
4. Pour 3 tablespoons of oil on a heavy-bottomed sauté pan and add the rolled meat cylinder on the hot oil.
5. Cook for 30 minutes until all the rouladen turns golden brown and place them in a large Dutch oven.
6. Heat 2 cups of water in a small pan and pour the hot water into the same heavy-bottomed sauté pan.
7. Scrape the drippings in the pan to form the gravy. Pour this gravy sauce over the meat in the Dutch oven.

8. Add water to cover 2/3rd of the meat and bring it to boil on a stovetop. Reduce the heat, cover and simmer on low for 1-½ hours.
9. When the meat is cooked and turns tender, transfer to a plate and cover it with foil.
10. Take a small bowl and whisk 1/4-cup water and 1/4 cup cornstarch until smooth and creamy.
11. Add 1/2 of the whisked cream to the Dutch oven (you will find the juices of the cooked meat remaining in it) and whisk again until the mixture is incorporated.
12. Turn on the heat and simmer until the mixture thickens. Add 1/4-cup sour cream before serving.
13. Transfer the rouladen pieces (one per plate) to the plate and pour the prepared gravy generously.
14. Serve with pasta, potatoes, corn or broccoli. Enjoy!

Kaese Spaetzle

Servings: 8

Ingredients:

- 3 eggs
- 1 sliced onion
- 1 1/2 cups all-purpose flour
- 1 1/2 cups Emmentaler cheese (shredded)
- 3/8 cup 2 percent milk
- 3/4 teaspoon nutmeg (ground)
- 3 tablespoons butter
- 3/4 teaspoon salt
- 1/8 teaspoon pepper

Method:

1. Sift the nutmeg, flour, pepper and salt together in a small bowl.
2. Take another medium bowl and beat the eggs well. Add the milk and flour mixture alternately to the eggs. Beat them until smooth and let it stand for 30 minutes.
3. Boil water and 1/2-teaspoon salt in a large pot. Press the prepared batter into the water through a Spaetzle press or potato ricer. Let it cook.
4. Remove the Spaetzle with a slotted spoon when it floats on top of the water to a bowl. Mix 1 cup of cheese to the cooked Spaetzle.
5. Take a large skillet and melt the butter over medium-high heat. Add the onion and cook until it turns golden brown.

6. Add the cheese-mixed Spaetzle to the skillet and mix well. You can add the remaining cheese (if any) and stir well until it blends well.
7. Transfer to a plate and serve immediately.

Sauerbraten

Servings: 8

Ingredients:

- 4 pounds chuck roast (trim the excess fat and pat dry)
- 2 chopped onions,
- 2 chopped celery ribs
- 4 chopped carrots
- 4 minced garlic cloves
- 1 cup dry red wine
- 1 cup gingersnap cookies (finely crushed)
- 3 tablespoons vegetable oil
- 1/2 teaspoon cloves (ground)
- 1/2 cup brown sugar
- 1/2 cup red wine vinegar
- 1 teaspoon salt
- 2 bay leaves
- 1/2 cup water
- 1 teaspoon pepper

Method:

1. Rub the salt and pepper over the roast and keep it aside.
2. Heat oil in a pressure cooker and cook the chuck roast until all the sides turn brown (use the *brown* function in the cooker or roast the meat without the lid if it is an old-fashioned cooker).
3. Take a small bowl and mix the wine, water, vinegar, bay leaves, cloves, salt and sugar until combined well.
4. Place the gingersnaps and chopped vegetables around the browned roast; pour the vinegar mixture over the entire contents.

5. Close the cooker, raise the pressure to high and let it cook for 50 minutes.
6. Let the pressure release naturally after the meat is done (don't manually release the pressure).
7. Open the lid when the pressure drops and transfer the meat (only the roast not the vegetables) to a plate. Remove the bay leaves and cover it with a foil.
8. Pour the cooked vegetables and sauce in a high-speed blender and blend until smooth.
9. Remove the foil of the meat and serve with the blended sauce.

Kartoffelpuffer

Servings: 5

Ingredients:

- 2 Eggs
- 7 medium starchy potatoes (grated)
- 1/3 cups Plain flour
- 1 grated brown onion
- 1 tablespoon butter
- 1 tablespoon olive oil
- 1/2 teaspoon Salt

Method:

1. Take a large bowl and mix the grated onions and potatoes.
2. Crack 2 eggs and lightly beat them.
3. Add the beaten eggs, 1/3 cup flour and salt to the bowl of grated onions and potatoes.
4. Mix together well until combined.
5. Heat the olive oil and butter in a frying pan.
6. Scoop out 1/4 cup of the mixture and flatten them a little bit.
7. Place this in the hot oil and fry for 5 minutes until both the side turn golden.
8. Drain on paper towels and serve with sauce. Enjoy!

Chicken Paprikash

Servings: 6

Ingredients:

- 6 chicken breasts (boneless and skinless)
- 1 chopped onion
- 1 1/2 cups chicken stock
- 4 minced garlic cloves
- 1/3 cup flour
- 2 teaspoons paprika
- 1 1/2 cups sour cream
- 3 tablespoons tomato paste
- 2 tablespoons peanut oil
- 1 tablespoon cornstarch
- 1 tablespoon butter
- 1 teaspoon salt
- 1 teaspoon smoked paprika
- 1/8 teaspoon white pepper

Method:

1. Take a shallow plate and mix the flour, pepper, 2 teaspoons paprika and salt until combined well. Dip the chicken breasts into the mixture and coat well on both sides.
2. Heat the butter and peanut oil in a heavy-bottomed skillet over medium heat. Add the coated chicken and cook for 5 minutes until both the sides turn brown.
3. Once all the chicken breasts are done, transfer to a plate and set aside.
4. Add the garlic and onion to the same skillet and stir-fry until they turn tender and crisp.

5. Add the tomato paste and the chicken stock into the skillet. Stir the contents until they combine well. Bring it to boil.
6. Place the cooked chicken back to the skillet and cover it with a lid. Lower the heat and simmer for 8 minutes.
7. Take another small bowl and mix the cornstarch, sour cream and the smoked paprika until they combine well.
8. Add this mixture into the skillet when the chicken is cooked thoroughly and heat through it (do not boil!)
9. Serve with hot cooked rice or mashed potatoes.

Basic Bread Stuffing

Servings: 6

Ingredients:

- 1 container chicken broth
- 1/4 cup finely chopped onions
- 2 beaten eggs
- 1/2 cup chopped celery
- 4 cups bread cubes
- 1/2 teaspoon poultry seasoning
- 1/3 cup butter
- 1/2 teaspoon sage
- 1/8 teaspoon black pepper
- 1/2 teaspoon salt

Method:

1. Preheat the oven to 325 F. Grease the baking dish with butter (be generous while greasing)
2. Heat butter in a frying pan over medium heat. Add onion and celery to the pan, sauté until the mixture softens.
3. Transfer the cooked onion-celery mixture into a large bowl. Add the bread cubes, poultry seasoning, sage, pepper and salt. Mix well until combined.
4. Add the broth to the mixture and stir until all the contents are moistened well. Check for taste and add salt accordingly.
5. Beat the eggs in a separate bowl and add it to the broth mixture. Stir until all the contents blend well.
6. Pour the batter into the greased baking dish. Pack it loosely and cover the dish with the foil tightly.
7. Bake for 40 minutes and then remove the foil.

8. Bake again for another 10 minutes until browned.
9. Serve hot.

Cheese Spätzle

Servings: 6

Ingredients:

- 3 cups Emmentaler cheese (shredded)
- 3 cups (12 ounces) dry Spätzle (cooked)
- 2 sliced small onions
- 2 tablespoon olive oil
- Salt and pepper to taste

Method:

1. Preheat the oven to 325 F.
2. Heat the olive oil in a skillet over medium heat. Add the onions and sauté for 10 minutes until it becomes translucent and brown.
3. Grease the casserole dish and layer with 1/2 Spätzle. Season with pepper and salt.
4. Prepare the next layer by sprinkling 1/2 of the shredded cheese and again another ½ layer Spätzle and end it with 1/2 layer of cheese.
5. Top the casserole with sautéed onions and back for 30 minutes uncovered.
6. You can transfer to a plate once the casserole becomes bubbly and turns brown on the top.
7. Serve warm and enjoy!

German Noodle Nests

Servings: 6

Ingredients:

- 1 pound quartered mushrooms (fresh)
- 12 ounces spaghetti
- 4 ounces cubed mozzarella
- 3 chopped green onions
- 2 precooked smoked sausage (cubed)
- 1 minced garlic clove
- 24 ounces pasta sauce (1 can)
- 5 tablespoons olive oil
- Salt, pepper to taste

Method:

1. Preheat oven to 400 F.
2. Cook the spaghetti in a pot as per the package instructions until it is firm to bite. Drain and rinse with cold water.
3. Transfer the spaghetti back to the pot and add 3 tablespoons of olive oil. Mix well and set aside.
4. Heat the remaining olive oil in a frying pan and add the mushrooms. Stir-fry until it browns.
5. Add the sausage to the pan and stir-fry until it turns brown. Add the garlic and onion; continue to stir-fry until tender and brown. Cook for few minutes and remove from heat.
6. Take a casserole dish and put 1/3 of pasta sauce to the bottom. Divide the spaghetti into 6 portions and form noodle nests.

7. Place a portion on a sauce and twirl it around with a fork from the nest with a depression in the center. Slide the nest into the casserole dish.
8. Repeat step 7 with the remaining spaghetti.
9. Pour the mushroom mixture into the center of the 7 nests and pour the remaining pasta sauce around the nests.
10. Sprinkle the mozzarella over the top and bake uncovered for 30 minutes until it turns bubbly.
11. Transfer to plate and serve hot.

Easy Asparagus

Servings: 6

Ingredients:

- 2 pounds fresh asparagus (washed and dried)
- 1/4 cup Parmesan cheese (ground)
- 1/2 cup bread crumbs (seasoned)
- 1 teaspoon freshly ground pepper
- 1/2 cup olive oil

Method:

1. Preheat oven to 400 F.
2. Pour 1/4 cup olive oil onto a cookie sheet (with rim).
3. Snap the bottom end of the dried asparagus and peel the stem if required.
4. Lay them neatly onto the cookie sheet.
5. Drizzle the oil over them all and gently turn the spring vegetable until they are completely coated with oil.
6. Sprinkle the breadcrumbs over them and then the ground Parmesan cheese.
7. Season with the freshly ground pepper and bake for 15 minutes until they turn crispy and fragrant.
8. Transfer to a plate and serve warm with any creamy dip.

Chapter Six: Traditional German Dinner Recipes

Bratkartoffeln

Servings: 4

Ingredients:

- 5 cups peeled and chopped potatoes
- 6 bacon pieces
- 1 finely chopped large onion
- 1 teaspoon paprika
- 2 tablespoons extra-virgin olive oil
- Salt and pepper, to taste

Method:

1. Heat 1 tablespoon of oil in a skillet over medium-high heat.
2. Place the 6 pieces of bacon on the hot oil and cook until browned. Reserve the bacon fat and transfer the cooked bacon to a plate.
3. Add the onions to the same skillet, which has bacon fat and some oil. Sauté for 3 minutes until the onions are soft and translucent.
4. Transfer the cooked onions to the plate that has the cooked bacon. Set aside
5. Add a small amount of chopped potatoes in a single layer in the same skillet. Add paprika, salt and pepper. Give it a stir and cover the skillet with a lid.
6. Cook on medium heat until the potatoes become soft. Flip them to the other side halfway through the cooking.

7. Repeat steps 5 and 6 with the remaining potatoes by adding 1 tablespoon of olive oil.
8. Transfer the fried potatoes to the plate of bacon and onions. Season it with more paprika, salt and pepper if needed.
9. Serve warm and enjoy!

Black Forest Inn Potato Purée

Servings: 2

Ingredients:

- 1 pound peeled and quartered Idaho potatoes
- 1 1/4 cups heavy cream (warmed)
- 1 stick butter (finely cubed)
- 1/4 teaspoon white pepper (ground)
- 1/2 teaspoon sea salt
- Pinch of ground nutmeg

Method:

1. Boil the potatoes in a large pot of water over medium-high heat until they are firm but tender. Drain and dry the cooked potatoes
2. Take a medium-sized bowl and pass the hot potatoes through a potato ricer.
3. Add the butter pieces and fold them in with the potatoes using a wooden spoon.
4. Add pepper, salt and nutmeg to the bowl. Mix well until blended.
5. Add the warmed cream bit by bit to the bowl and slowly whisk the contents using a hand blender but don't overwork the mixture.
6. Add more cream if needed to reach the required puree consistency. Season with more pepper and salt if required
7. Put the hot potato cream mixture into a pastry bag and pipe it onto the plates.
8. Serve warm and enjoy.

Braised Red Cabbage

Servings: 8

Ingredients:

- 2 red cabbage heads (quartered and thinly sliced)
- 2 tablespoons bacon grease
- 1 large onion (peeled, halved and sliced)
- 1 large Granny Smith apple (cored and cut in 8)
- 1/4 cup red wine vinegar
- 1 tablespoon brown sugar
- 1/2 cup dry red wine
- 1/2 teaspoon ground cloves
- Salt and pepper, as per taste
- 1 teaspoon ground cinnamon
- 2 tablespoons butter (optional)
- 2 cups water

Method:

1. Heat the bacon grease in a large skillet over medium-high heat.
2. Add the onions, cabbage and apples to the hot grease. Stir well until the contents are completely coated.
3. Add the red wine vinegar, brown sugar, dry red wine, cloves, cinnamon, salt and pepper to the skillet.
4. Stir well until well incorporated.
5. Add 2 cups of water and bring it to boil.
6. Reduce the heat to medium-low, cover the skillet and simmer for 45 minutes until the cabbages become soft and tender.

7. If it is too watery, remove the lid for the liquid to evaporate as the cabbage must not be too soupy but moist.
8. Add 2 tablespoons of butter and give the entire contents a good nice stir.
9. Transfer to a plate and serve hot.

Edel-Labskaus

Servings: 6

Ingredients:

- 14 ounces red beets (washed and unpeeled)
- 2 ounces finely diced gherkins
- 9 ounces peeled potatoes
- 2 peeled and finely diced shallots
- 1 bunch dill (finely chopped)
- 1/3 cup milk
- 1 teaspoon finely diced orange peel
- 1/2 cup red beet juice
- 6 tablespoons cold-pressed canola oil
- 2 ounces butter
- 2 tablespoons vinegar
- 2 tablespoons fruit vinegar
- 1 tablespoon + 1 teaspoon caraway seeds
- Salt and pepper, to taste
- Sugar

Method:

1. Place the beets in a pot of salted water with a little sugar, splash of vinegar and 1 tablespoon caraway seeds.
2. Cook them for 15 minutes until the beets become tender. Turn off heat and let it cool.
3. Peel the beets, dice them and set aside
4. Wash the pot and boil the peeled potatoes in salted water until soft and tender. Drain the cooked potatoes and set aside.

5. Melt the butter in a large pan over medium heat. Reserve 2 tablespoons of diced beets and add the rest to the melted butter.
6. Stir well as you add the beet juice, orange peel, milk and 1 teaspoon caraway seeds to the pan.
7. Bring the contents to boil and add the cooked potatoes. Reduce the heat to lowest and mash the mixture coarsely using a potato masher.
8. Now, add the fruit vinegar, diced shallots, canola oil, gherkins and the reserved beets to the pan.
9. Add the dill, pepper and salt to the mixture. Stir well until the contents are incorporated well.
10. Let it simmer for few minutes and then turn off the heat
11. Transfer to a plate and serve hot. This goes well with the potato puree (the recipe mentioned at the beginning of this chapter).

Fried Asparagus with Herb Cream

Servings: 4-6

Ingredients:

- 1 1/2 pounds white asparagus
- 1 hard-boiled egg (chopped)
- 2 tablespoons parsley (chopped)
- 1 cup all-purpose flour
- 1 egg separated
- 5 fluid ounces light German beer
- 2 German pickles (chopped)
- 1 1/2 cups mayonnaise
- 1 small onion (chopped)
- 2 tablespoons chives (chopped)
- 1 tablespoon canola oil
- 1 tablespoon butter
- Mustard
- Salt and pepper, to taste
- Lemon juice

Method:

1. Wash the asparagus thoroughly and peel them. Chop the woody ends and cut the stems into 2.5 inch-pieces. Cook these pieces in boiling water for 8 minutes and then drain. Let it cool and pat dry with paper towels.
2. Take a large bowl and combine the flour, beer, oil, salt and egg yolk. Whisk them together and let the batter sit for 30 minutes.
3. Take a small bowl and beat the egg white nicely until it becomes stiff. Mix this to the beer-flour batter until combined. Set aside.

4. Spoon the mayonnaise to a small bowl and add the chopped eggs, onions and pickle to the bowl. Mix it well until combined. Now, add the parsley, chives, mustard, lemon juice, salt and pepper to the mayonnaise mixture. Mix well until blended thoroughly. Cover and refrigerate for 20 minutes.
5. Melt the butter in a frying pan over medium-high heat. Dip the asparagus pieces into the beer-egg batter and place it over the melted butter in the frying pan.
6. Shallow-fry until golden brown and transfer to a plate.
7. Serve hot with cold herb cream (remove the mayonnaise cream from the refrigerator).

Herbed Spaetzle

Servings: 8

Ingredients:

- 2 boxes German Spaetzle
- 1 tablespoon flat-leaf parsley (chopped)
- 3 tablespoons butter
- 1 teaspoon freshly ground whole white peppercorns
- 1 tablespoon chives (chopped)
- Sea salt, as per taste
- 1 pinch ground nutmeg

Method:

1. Cook the German Spaetzle as per the directions mentioned in the package and set aside in a large bowl
2. Heat the butter in a saucepan over medium heat and continue to cook the melted butter until it turns nut-colored brown.
3. Pour the browned butter over the hot Spaetzle. Add the chives, nutmeg, salt, parsley and white paper to the buttered Spaetzle. Give it a nice toss until the flavors are blended well.
4. Transfer to a plate and serve warm.

Horseradish-Roasted Fall Vegetables

Servings: 6

Ingredients:

- 2 tablespoons creamy German horseradish
- 3 pound chopped red potatoes
- 1 large crisp apple (cored and chopped)
- 1 medium acorn squash
- 2 tablespoons olive oil
- Salt and pepper, to taste

Method:

1. Preheat oven to 375 degrees F
2. Keep the squash in the oven for 10 minutes to soften. Remove from oven, peel, discard the seeds and cut into bite-sized pieces.
3. Take a small bowl and combine the oil, horseradish cream, salt and pepper. Whisk them together until creamy and smooth.
4. Roast the apple and potatoes in a pan and add the chopped squash to it.
5. Pour the horseradish cream mixture over the vegetables and toss it until the veggies are coated well with the cream.
6. Continue to roast for an hour without covering the pan and tossing once in a while.
7. When the veggies are deeply roasted and caramelized, transfer to a plate.
8. Serve hot and enjoy!

Farmer's Omelet

Servings: 4

Ingredients:

- 10 ounces cold cooked potatoes (sliced with medium thickness)
- 5 beaten and seasoned large eggs
- 4 ounces bacon
- 1 large Bierwurst
- 2 ounces Bavarian Emmentaler cheese
- 1 teaspoon sea salt
- 1 teaspoon pepper (freshly ground)
- 2 tablespoons canola oil
- A handful of croutons (optional)

Method:

1. Heat 1 tablespoon of oil in heavy-bottomed non-stick frying pan over medium heat.
2. Add the bacon and fry until crisp. Drain on a paper towel and set aside.
3. Slice the Bierwurst sausage into half lengthwise (thick on the diagonal). Fry these slices in the same pan until they turn crisp and golden. Drain them on a paper towel and set aside.
4. Add the remaining oil in the same pan and heat it. Sauté the sliced potatoes in the pan until they turn golden brown.
5. Add the sausage and bacon to the pan along with the potatoes. If you are using the croutons, you will need to scatter them on top of the contents now.

6. Stir the contents until they are combined thoroughly. Pour the beaten eggs into the pan and stir lightly as you tip the pan for the liquid egg to settle evenly.
7. Once the eggs are done, scatter the cheese and fork lightly in. Turn down the heat and cook slowly for 15 minutes. The top needs to set.
8. Remove from heat and let the contents in the pan sit for 5 minutes.
9. Use a palette knife to cut the omelet and transfer to a plate.
10. Serve warm with sauce.

Dijon-Dill Chicken and Noodles

Servings: 2

Ingredients:

- 1/2 cup wide egg noodles (uncooked)
- 40 ounces finely sliced chicken breast (boneless skinless)
- 2 cups broccoli florets (fresh)
- 1 medium onion (chopped)
- 10 ounces cream cheese (fat-free)
- 18.5 ounces Progresso Light vegetable and noodle soup (1 can)
- 1/8 teaspoon dill weed (dried)
- 2 tablespoons Dijon mustard

Method:

1. Cook the onion and chicken in a 12-inch nonstick skillet over medium-high heat.
2. Keep stirring continuously until the chicken starts to turn brown and the onions become tender.
3. Add the soup, dill weed and mustard to the skillet. Stir until the contents combine well and bring it to boil.
4. Reduce heat and add the noodles while you continue to stir. Bring it to boil again.
5. Reduce the heat to medium, cover the skillet and cook for 6 minutes stirring occasionally.
6. Add the broccoli and cook uncovered for 4 more minutes. Keep stirring frequently until the florets turn crisp tender.
7. Add the cream and cheese into the mixture until they blend well.
8. Transfer to a plate and serve hot.

Sauerkraut Potato Pizza with Cauliflower Crust

Servings: 6 slices

Ingredients:

- 1/2 cup sauerkraut
- 1 pound cauliflower rice
- 1 cup thinly sliced potatoes
- 1 1/4 cup shredded vegan mozzarella cheese (Daiya brand or similar)
- 1/2 cup almond flour
- 1 finely minced garlic clove
- 1/4 teaspoon red pepper flakes
- 3 tablespoons flax seeds (ground), divided
- 3 tablespoons water

Method:

1. Preheat the oven to 400 F.
2. Take a small bowl and mix 2 tablespoons of ground flax seeds with 3 tablespoons of water until combined well. Set it aside to thicken and form a *thick flax egg*.
3. Place the cauliflower rice into a 2-quart saucepan and add water to cover the rice completely.
4. Bring it to boil, cover the saucepan and reduce the heat to simmer. Let it cook for 5 more minutes.
5. Drain the liquid and transfer the cooked cauliflower rice to a bowl (freezer-safe). Freeze it for 10 minutes.
6. Remove from freezer and transfer the rice to the center of a clean linen dish tower. Wrap the tower around the cauliflower and patiently drain out all the moisture you can. (Wring out).

7. Now, take a large bowl and place the cauliflower rice in it. Add the *thick flax egg,* remaining flaxseeds, minced garlic and almond flour. Mix them altogether.
8. Transfer the mixture to the center of a parchment-lined baking sheet and shape it to the desired size. Let the crust be 1/4 inch thick and form a little rim on the edge (there shouldn't be any bare spots).
9. Mix 1/4 of lukewarm water with 3-tablespoon salt in a medium ball. When the salt is completely incorporated, place the sliced potatoes into the salt water. Let it soak for 30 minutes.
10. Now, bake the cauliflower crust for 30 minutes until it browns well on the top. Keep a close check on it. Remove from the oven.
11. Drain the potatoes and rinse well. Spin them dry using a salad spinner.
12. Take another bowl and mix the potato slices with mozzarella shreds, sauerkraut and onion. Place this mixture evenly on the baked cauliflower crust. Sprinkle the red pepper flakes on the top.
13. Bake the crust in a preheated 400 degrees F oven for 20 minutes. The cheese should melt and the potatoes should turn brown.
14. Slice the pizza using a pizza cutter.
15. Transfer to the plate and serve warm. Top it with more cheese or pepper flakes if you desire.

Cheesy Spaetzle with Vegetables

Servings: 2

Ingredients:

- 4 eggs
- 1 cup cherry tomatoes (sliced into half)
- 3 peeled and shredded carrots (big)
- 7/8 cup peas
- 1/3 cup Emmentaler cheese (grated)
- 1 chopped onion (big)
- 10 tablespoons all-purpose flour
- 3 tablespoons butter
- 1 tablespoon pepper (freshly ground)
- 1 tablespoon Salt
- 1 teaspoon nutmeg

Method:

1. Preheat the oven to 400 F.
2. Take a large bowl and mix the eggs (crack it), flour, salt, nutmeg and 3/8 cup water. Stir briskly until bubbles start to form. Let the dough sit for 15 minutes.
3. Boil water with a bit of salt in a big pot. Place the dough on a Spaetzle board and scrape it off slowly into the water using a scraper.
4. The Spaetzle gets cooked in 3 minutes, remove them from water and rinse with cold water (this stops them from getting cooked further).
5. Set the cooked Spaetzle in an oven-safe dish.
6. Heat the butter in a skillet and add the carrots, peas, pepper, tomatoes and onion into it. Cook for 3 minutes and flavor it with pepper and salt.

7. Add the cooked vegetables in the Spaetzle and mix well. Sprinkle the cheese over it and place the dish in the oven.
8. Bake for 5-10 minutes until the cheese melts.
9. Transfer to a plate and serve hot.

Polish Sausage Supper

Servings: 4

Ingredients:

- 1 ring fully cooked smoked sausage (sliced into 1-inch pieces)
- 1 slightly beaten egg
- 1 large Granny Smith apple (peeled and sliced into eight pieces)
- 1 1/2 cups Original Bisquick pancake and baking mix
- 15 ounces drained sauerkraut (1 can)
- 1/2 cup milk
- 1 cup apple juice
- 1/2 cup Cheddar cheese (shredded)
- 1 tablespoon fresh parsley (chopped)

Method:

1. Preheat oven to 425 degrees F
2. Layer the apple and sausage in a 2-quart glass baking dish (ungreased).
3. Top it with sauerkraut and pour the apple juice over the layered contents.
4. Cover with foil and bake for 40 minutes until you can pierce the apple pieces with a fork.
5. Remove the baking dish and set it aside.
6. Take a small bowl and mix the egg, baking mix, milk, cheddar cheese and parsley together until you can form a soft dough.
7. Spoon the dough and drop it onto the sausage mixture (8 spoons).
8. Bake for 12 minutes uncovered until the biscuits turn golden brown and are completely cooked.

9. Transfer to a plate and serve warm.

Potato-Chickpea Patties with Porcini Mushrooms

Servings: 4

Ingredients:

- 3/8 cup instant mashed potatoes with chickpeas
- 1/8 pound porcini mushrooms (dried)
- 3 tablespoons rapeseed oil
- 7/8 cups almond milk
- 1 bunch of chives (cleaned and chopped)
- Salt

Method:

1. Take a bowl and place the porcini mushrooms in them. Add boiling water to the mushrooms and let it soak for 10 minutes. Chop them into small pieces when the mushrooms become soft.
2. Take another bowl and mix the instant mashed potatoes-chickpeas with almond milk. Let it soak for 5 minutes.
3. Now, add the mushroom and chopped chives to the potato mixture. Season with salt. Mix the contents well until it combines thoroughly.
4. Heat the rapeseed oil a skillet over medium heat.
5. Take a spoon of the mixture and place it in your left hand (grease hands with water or oil). Flatten the mixture to make a patty. (You can also scoop a tablespoon into the pan directly and flatten it make a patty).
6. Place the patty in the hot oil and fry until golden brown on both sides.
7. Drain the oil by keeping the fried patties in paper towels.

8. Transfer to a plate and serve warm with sauce.

Quinoa Sushi

Servings: 4

Ingredients:

- 7/8 cups quinoa (multi-colored)
- 6 spinach leaves
- 1/2 cup tofu (sliced into strips)
- 3 nori seaweed sheets
- 1 teaspoon agave
- Several carrot strips
- 1 teaspoon soy sauce
- Several pickle strips
- 1 tablespoon rapeseed oil
- Several chive sprigs
- 1 tablespoon rice vinegar
- 2 cups water
- Salt

Method:

1. Add quinoa, water and a dash of salt in a pot. Bring the contents to boil and simmer for 15 minutes until the quinoa has soaked up the water.
2. Add rice vinegar and agave to the pot and stir well until the contents are mixed well. Let the mixture cool for some time.
3. Heat the rapeseed oil in a small skit over medium heat. Place the tofu strips in the oil and fry until crispy.
4. Transfer the fried tofu to a plate and pour the soy sauce over it until they are covered with the sauce.
5. Place the spinach in a colander and pour boiling water over them for the leaves to get soft.

6. Now, blanch the carrot strips for a minute. Take a bamboo sushi mate and place one sheet nori in the center.
7. Place 1/3rd of the quinoa on the nori sheet and spread it out until 3/4th of the sheet is covered (make sure you leave 1/4th of the sheet exposed).
8. Place 2 chive sprigs, 2 spinach leaves, pickle strips, one tofu strip and one carrot strip on the quinoa mixture. Roll the nori sheet with the help of bamboo sushi mat and seal the roll (1/4th of the open side of nori sheet) with water.
9. Make 2 more rolls and cut each roll into 6 pieces. Serve with soy sauce.

Sausage Skewers with Mango and Bell Pepper

Servings: 4

Ingredients:

- 6 Meica sausages (cut into one-inch pieces)
- 1 mango (peeled and chopped into 1x1 inch pieces)
- 1 chopped bell pepper (deseeded)
- 2 tablespoons olive oil for frying
- Wooden skewers

Method:

1. Take a skewer and put a mango piece, sausage and bell pepper piece in an alternating pattern.
2. Place the skewers on the grill and cook until they are brown on all the sides.
3. You can also fry the skewers in a huge skillet.
4. Transfer them to a plate and relish.

Roasted Potatoes

Servings: 6

Ingredients:

- 7 potatoes (big)
- 1 cup diced bacon or ham (ignore this ingredient if you want to make the dish vegetarian)
- 1/2 onion (sliced)
- 2 tablespoons re-solidified butter
- 1 1/2 teaspoon salt
- 1 teaspoon black pepper

Method:

1. Boil the potatoes and peel the skin off. Cut them into thick half-inch slices.
2. Heat the re-solidified butter in a skillet over medium heat.
3. Place the sliced potatoes in the pan and ensure they don't overlap.
4. Fry until they turn golden brown on both the sides. Season with salt and check the taste.
5. Add the sliced onion and stir-fry until they turn brown and soft.
6. Transfer to a plate and sprinkle black pepper over the roasted potatoes.
7. Serve hot
8. If you are using meat, then add the meat after step 5 and cook until it browns.
9. Add more salt if required and mix well.
10. Transfer to a plate and serve with hot sauce.

Creamed Kohlrabi

Servings: 2

Ingredients:

- 2 finely sliced kohlrabi (peel it first before slicing)
- 1/4 cup flaked butter
- 1/4 cup heavy cream
- Dash of sugar
- Salt and pepper, to taste
- 1 tablespoon fresh cilantro leaves (chopped)

Method:

1. Add the kohlrabi and heavy cream in a pot and heat it up.
2. Add salt, pepper and a dash of sugar to the contents and mix well.
3. Cook for 10 minutes until the vegetable becomes soft.
4. Add the flaked butter and cover the pot. Simmer for 8 minutes until the contents are cooked well.
5. Transfer to a plate and garnish with the chopped cilantro.
6. Serve hot and enjoy!

Chapter Seven: Traditional German Dessert Recipes

Dark Chocolate Cherry Cupcakes with Kirsch Frosting

Servings: 12 cups

Ingredients:

- 1 bar German dark chocolate chopped (3 1/2-ounce)
- 1 cup frozen unsweetened cherries (unthawed and sliced into half) or fresh pitted cherries
- 1 large egg
- 4 tablespoons softened butter (unsalted)
- 1 cup + 1 tablespoon all-purpose flour
- 2 tablespoons German Kirschwasser cherry brandy
- 2 cups sifted confectioner's sugar
- 1 stick softened butter (unsalted)
- 1 tablespoon milk
- 3/4 cup sour cream
- 1/2 teaspoon baking soda
- 1/4 teaspoon salt
- 1 drop red food coloring
- 3/4 cup sugar
- 1 teaspoon vanilla
- Fresh cherries (for garnishing)

Method:

1. Preheat oven to 350 F.
2. Line 12 muffin cups with paper liners and set them aside.

3. Melt the chocolate in a double boiler (place the chocolate bars on top of the boiler over simmering water until it melts).
4. Take a medium-sized bowl and whisk together the baking soda, 1-cup flour and salt. Set this aside.
5. Take another large bowl and add the butter and sugar. Beat using a hand mixer for 2 minutes at medium speed until it becomes fluffy. Add the egg, vanilla and sour cream to the bowl and beat well.
6. Now add the melted chocolate and the flour mixture. Beat at low speed until the contents are combined well.
7. Take a plate and place the remaining 1-tablespoon of flour in it. Toss the cherries in the flour.
8. Add the flour-tossed cherries into the batter and stir well. Spoon the batter into the 12 muffin cups.
9. Bake for 22 minutes until the cupcake becomes soft and spongy (use a wooden toothpick and insert to the center of the cupcake, if it comes out clean the cupcake is ready).
10. Cook the cupcakes in a pan on a wire rack for 5 minutes.
11. Take another large bowl and beat the 1 stick butter, milk, confectioners' sugar and cherry brandy with a hand mixer at medium speed until smooth.
12. Add the drop of food coloring and beat it again until it blends well.
13. Spread the frosting over the cupcakes.
14. Serve and enjoy!

Hazelnut Crown

Servings: 4

Ingredients:

- 3 cups hazelnuts (ground)
- 9 fresh eggs (medium ones)
- 2/3 cup walnuts (ground)
- 1 fresh egg white (medium ones)
- 2 cups sifted powdered sugar
- 1 1/2 cups sugar
- Yellow food color
- 1 pinch Salt
- Some sugar flowers

Method:

1. Preheat oven at 160F
2. Separate 5 eggs. Beat the separated yolks and the remaining 4 whole eggs until creamy white.
3. Add some salt in the separated egg whites and beat it until it becomes stiff.
4. Mix the hazelnuts, walnuts and the beaten egg whites together. Now fold this mixture into the egg yolk cream.
5. Take an 8-cup ring-shaped cake form and pour the batter into it such that $3/4^{th}$ of it is full, as the dough will rise while baking.
6. Bake for 60 minutes in the preheated oven. Once done, remove the cake from the mold and cool it on a wire rack.
7. Take another bowl and pour the 1 remaining egg white into it. Add the sifted powdered sugar and mix well.

8. Take 4 tablespoons of the mixed glaze and tint it with yellow food coloring. Put this glaze in the freezer safe bag and set it aside.
9. Layer the cake with the remaining white glaze and allow it to dry.
10. Now cut the tip of the freezer safe bag and pipe the yellow glaze in thick lines and make a yellow petal pattern. Decorate with sugar flowers when the glaze is still wet.
11. Refrigerate it for an hour and serve chilled. Or you can also serve immediately.

Marzipan Jubilee Torte

Servings: 20

Ingredients:

- 12 eggs
- 10 1/2 ounces melted couverture chocolate glaze (semi sweet)
- 4 1/4 ounces chopped chocolate (semi-sweet)
- 2 cups vanilla pudding mix (Dr. Oetker brand)
- 4 cups milk
- Niederegger marzipan loaf without chocolate (18 ounces)
- 17 ounces butter (2 sticks + 1 tablespoon in room temperature)
- Pulp from 2 vanilla beans
- 3 ounces all-purpose flour (sifted)
- 4 teaspoon sugar (granulated)
- 3 ounces sugar (non- granulated)
- 2 cups powdered sugar

Method:

1. Preheat oven to 350 F.
2. Beat 4 eggs and 1-ounce sugar for 7 minutes until it becomes foamy.
3. Fold 2 tablespoons sifted flour and 6 tablespoons chopped chocolates thrice into the beaten egg mixture.
4. Cover three baking trays with wax paper and set aside.
5. Spread the mixed dough onto the three trays and bake for 15 minutes until it turns golden brown.

6. Turn the biscuit layers from the trays onto cloths and spread with granulated sugar (to avoid sticking). Remove the wax paper and let it cool.
7. Prepare the vanilla cream pudding by adding milk and sugar to the mixture as directed in the package.
8. Scrape the pulp and seeds from the vanilla beans and add it to the pudding while it is hot. Once done, let it cool for some time.
9. Now add the room temperature butter with a tablespoon to the pudding and stir well (be careful while adding the butter, you have to add it bit by bit slowly while you keep stirring).
10. Knead the marzipan loaf and powdered sugar together and roll the dough to the size of a baking tray.
11. Spread the $1/3^{rd}$ of the buttercream onto the first biscuit layer, then add the second biscuit layer and spread out the next $1/3^{rd}$ of buttercream filling. Finally add the third biscuit layer and spread the last third of the buttercream.
12. Place the marzipan layer on top and coat with melted chocolate.
13. Refrigerate for 2 hours and slice into 20 pieces.
14. Serve with edible leaf gold (if desired).

Tart Cherry Ice Cream

Servings: 4

Ingredients:

- 2 1/2 cups tart cherry fruit spread
- 2 eggs
- 1/4 cup cherry brandy
- 16 ounces fresh cream (not ultra-pasteurized)
- 2 egg yolks
- 1/2 cup sugar

Method:

1. Mix the sugar, egg yolks and eggs in a food processor for 10 minutes at high speed until it becomes frothy. Pour this into a big bowl.
2. Take another bowl and add the fresh cream. Whisk the cream until it turns stiff.
3. Add the cherry brandy and tart cherry fruit spread slowly to the cream. Whisk again.
4. Carefully fold the tart cherry cream mixture into the sugar-egg mixture.
5. Pour this mixture into a form and freeze it for 24 hours.
6. Serve chilled.

Tangerine Coconut Cake

Servings: 8

Ingredients:

- 3 eggs
- 1 cup grated coconut
- 1 Pack Kathi Lemon Cake mix
- 17.6 ounces tangerines (1 can)
- 1/2 cup heavy whipping cream
- 9.5 ounces butter
- 3/4 tablespoon water

Method:

1. Drain the tangerines well and reserve the juice.
2. Prepare the lemon cake by following the directions mentioned in the Kathi Lemon Cake mix. You will need to use eggs, butter and water along with the lemon cake mix to make the dough. Grease a 10-inch springform pan and pour the cake dough evenly into it.
3. Take another pan and melt the butter in it. Add the grated coconut, heavy whipping cream and 4 tablespoons tangerine juice to the heated butter. Mix until it blends thoroughly. Fold the tangerines carefully and spread it on the cake evenly.
4. Bake (as directed in the Kathi lemon cake mix) for 65 minutes until the cakes become soft and spongy. (A toothpick should go in and come out clean).
5. Cover the cakes with parchment paper after 50 minutes to prevent the cake from getting burnt.
6. Once done, let it cool.
7. Refrigerate for an hour, slice it and serve chilled.

Pumpernickel Ice Cream with Cranberries

Servings: 3

Ingredients:

- 2 ounces dark German chocolate
- 3 fresh eggs
- 2 ounces slightly dried Pumpernickel bread
- 1 cup heavy cream
- 4 tablespoons sugar
- 1/2 teaspoon vanilla extract
- Cranberries (for garnishing)

Method:

1. Grate the pumpernickel and chocolate together in a bowl and set it aside.
2. Take a small bowl and mix the sugar with the vanilla extract. Let it sit for some time.
3. Separate the eggs and blend the egg yolk with the sugar-vanilla mixture in a blender. Set the mixture aside.
4. Whip the egg whites separately in a bowl until it turns creamy.
5. Whip the cream in a separate bowl.
6. Fold the egg whites into the egg yolk mixture carefully. Now add the pumpernickel mixture and the cream.
7. Freeze for 4 hours.
8. Transfer to a bowl and serve with cranberries.

King of Hearts

Servings: 4

Ingredients:

- 4 small Gingerbread hearts
- 3 ounces Lebkuchen Gingerbread Rounds
- 3 scoops chocolate ice cream
- 2 1/2 cups 2 percent milk
- 2 tablespoons grated German chocolate
- 2 tablespoons confectioner's sugar

Method:

1. Place the Lebkuchen Gingerbread Rounds in a bowl and pour milk over them. Let it sit for 30 minutes until the gingerbread rounds soften.
2. Transfer this milk-Lebkuchen mixture into a high-speed blender.
3. Add ice cream and confectioners' sugar into the blender and blend on high speed until the lebkuchen are reduced to small pieces.
4. Pour this ice cream mixture into decorative bowls and decorate with grated German chocolate.
5. Serve chilled.

Fruit Pudding

Servings: 4

Ingredients:

- 1/4 cup cornstarch
- 2 pounds ripe fruit (strawberries, cranberries, raspberries, cherries, red or black currants) – *use at least 2 types of fruit*
- 3 cups water
- 1/2 cup sugar (granulated)

Method:

1. Wash and get the fruit ready. Remove pits if using cherries and chop the berries into easy-to-bite sizes.
2. Take a large pot and mix the fruit and water. Allow it to cook in low heat until the fruit become tender.
3. Take a sieve lined with cheesecloth and place it over a large bowl.
4. Pour the cooked fruit into the sieve. Don't crush the fruit.
5. Place the fruit in a large dish.
6. Boil the drained water over medium heat until it becomes a juice.
7. Take a small bowl and mix the cornstarch with cold water.
8. Add this to the hot juice and stir continuously. Add the sugar as per your taste and mix until combined well.
9. Pour this thickened juice over the fruit in the plate. Sprinkle lightly with sugar.
10. Refrigerate for 2 or 3 hours and serve.

German milchreis

Servings: 3

Ingredients:

- 3 cups milk
- 1 cup thick cream
- 1 cup short-grain white rice
- 1 teaspoon vanilla extract
- 1/4 cup sugar
- 1/8 teaspoon salt
- 1/2 teaspoon cinnamon
- Sugar to taste
- Fruit compote (optional)

Method:

1. Take a large saucepan and mix the rice, salt and sugar.
2. Now, add the milk and vanilla extract.
3. Heat the mixture over medium heat and bring it to boil.
4. Keep stirring frequently and once it comes to boil, reduce the heat.
5. Simmer for 30 minutes until the rice is cooked and the milk starts to thicken.
6. Continue stirring and remove the pan when the pudding is ready.
7. Transfer to a bowl and sprinkle a bit of sugar and cinnamon.
8. Serve warm. (You can also serve with fruit compote).

Conclusion

We have come to the end of this book. I would like to take this opportunity to thank you once again for choosing this book.

The book has covered the primary objective, which is to serve as a simple cookbook for any individual who wants to explore his or her meal choices with authentic and traditional German dishes. The chapters concentrate on a complete meal schedule ranging from breakfast to dessert – there are traditional recipes for lunch and dinner, which are mostly quick and easy to make.

Most flavors of German-based food will include cabbage, sauerkraut, onions, sausages, root vegetables, paprika, smoked meat, apples, dill, cream, caraway, butter and beer. Sausages are likely considered to be the most famous German food! The recipes mentioned here are traditionally German and some of them are simplified versions of the original cuisine.

I sincerely hope this book was useful and has helped in answering most of the queries you had in mind.

So, what are you waiting for? Try all the recipes mentioned in the book and enjoy mealtime with your entire family.

Thank you and best wishes!

Other Books by Grizzly Publishing

"Jamaican Cookbook: Traditional Jamaican Recipes Made Easy"

https://www.amazon.com/dp/B07B68KL8D

"Brazilian Instant Pot Cookbook: Delicious Pressure Cooked Meals Made Fast and Easy"

https://www.amazon.com/dp/B078XBYP89

"Norwegian Cookbook: Traditional Scandinavian Recipes Made Easy"

https://www.amazon.com/dp/B079M2W223

"Casserole Cookbook: Delicious Casserole Recipes From Around The World"

https://www.amazon.com/dp/B07B6GV61Q

Printed by Libri Plureos GmbH in Hamburg, Germany